THE MUSIC KIT

THE MUSIC KIT

THIRD EDITION

TOM MANOFF

Rhythm Reader and Scorebook

W · W · NORTON & COMPANY · New York · London

Third Edition

The text of this book is composed in Optima
Composition by David Budmen, Willow Graphics, Woodstown, NJ
Manufacturing by Courier, Westford
Book design by Jack Meserole

ISBN 0-393-96325-X   0-393-96327-6 (Apple II)   0-393-96330-6 (Macintosh)
    0-393-96328-4 (IBM 3.5")   0-393-96329-2 (IBM 5.25")

W. W. Norton & Company, Inc., 500 Fifth Avenue, New York, N.Y. 10110
W. W. Norton & Company Ltd., 10 Coptic Street, London WC1A 1PU

    6 7 8 9 0

Contents

Rhythm Reader

Contents

Scorebook

Rhythm Reader

CHAPTER ONE

Rhythm, Beat and Tempo

Rhythm is action in time. Whether the action is the sound of a symphony, the crash of a cymbal, or the ticking of a clock, it has a specific rhythm that occurs within time. **Rhythmic notation** is the system we use to indicate the number of actions in music, the amount of time each action takes, and the relationship of these actions to a basic ongoing pulse, called the **beat**. This beat is what we feel when we step in time to a marching band or tap our feet to a catchy tune. The **tempo**, or speed, of the beat can vary considerably. A polka has a fast tempo; a funeral march, a slow tempo. The rhythms we *hear* are represented by symbols we *see*; these are called **notes**.

Quarter Note and Eighth Note

The first notes we will learn are the quarter note (♩ or ♩) and the eighth note (♪ or ♪). Quarter notes are twice as long in duration as eighth notes; conversely, two eighth notes equal the duration of one quarter note.

$$♩ = ♪ ♪$$

The several parts of the eighth note are the **notehead**, **stem**, and **flag**:

stem ⟶ ♪ ⟵ flag
notehead ⟶

Beaming Eighth Notes

Eighth notes can be beamed together for easier reading.

beam

♪ ♪ = ♫

♪ ♪ ♪ ♪ = ♫♫

beam

1   Rewrite these eighth notes, using beams.

Example

a.

b.

c.

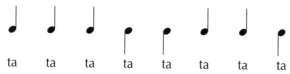

Speaking Rhythms   We will use an easy method for speaking simple rhythms: for quarter notes (♩ or ♩) we will say "ta," and for eighth notes (♪, ♪, ♫, or ♫) we will say "tee."

2   Speak in an even, steady manner, and at a moderate tempo.

ta   ta   ta   ta   ta   ta   ta   ta

Speak in an even, steady manner.

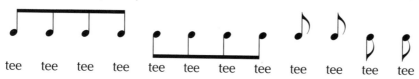

tee   tee   tee   tee   tee   tee   tee   tee   tee   tee   tee   tee

This method is effective as a short-term introduction to rhythmic notation. But once you have learned a rhythm using the spoken syllables, it is important to tap or clap the rhythm without them. You will most often be asked to tap or clap in this text.

3 a. Listen to *Rhythm 1* (Cassette) a few times, then speak the rhythm with the recording. Before each exercise, a count establishes the tempo. For this example, the count is "One, two, three, four."

b. Repeat *Rhythm 1*, speaking and following the version below; it is the same rhythm as the one above, but notated differently.

Double Bar   A **double bar** (‖ or 𝄁) indicates the end, as in exercise #3, above.

Repeat Signs   A group of notes is repeated when it is enclosed by **repeat signs**, ‖: :‖.
                      For example:

is performed

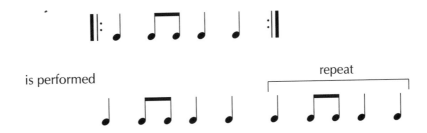

Sometimes the repeat sign appears only at the end of a group of notes or section of a piece. For example:

is performed

repeat

---

4 Write out each of these rhythms with the repeat.

Example

a.

b.

c.

When performing a line of music that repeats, go back to the beginning without any lapse of the beat when you reach the repeat sign.

5 Speak *Rhythms 1* through *3* with the cassette. Remember to observe the repeat signs.

a. *Rhythm 1:*

b. *Rhythm 2*:

c. *Rhythm 3*. You will hear "One, two, three" before the rhythm:

6 Repeat *Rhythms 1* through *3* with the cassette. This time tap or clap. Don't speak. Follow the notation in exercise #5, above.

7 Repeat *Rhythms 1* through *3* with the cassette. The versions below sound the same as in exercise #5, but are notated differently. Speak and clap.

a. *Rhythm 1*:

b. *Rhythm 2*:

c. *Rhythm 3*:

8 Do these on your own. Speak first, then clap or tap the rhythms on a table or a desk.

a.

b.

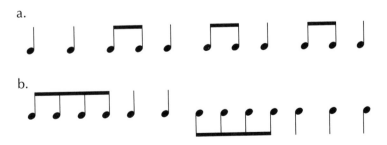

9   Tap these rhythms. Don't speak!

a.

b.

c.

d.

Fermata Sign

The **fermata** symbol (⌢), when placed above or below a note, indicates that the note is to be held for a longer duration than its normal value. The exact duration is left to the discretion of the performer. The fermata is sometimes called a **hold**.

Notes Control Space

The written note controls a space on the page in the same way that the sound it represents controls a period of time. To represent this relationship between time (sound) and space (notation), we will use a "Rhythm Spacer," a grid that shows how much space and time different notes take up. We will see that notes of longer duration control more space on the page than those of shorter duration.

The value of each box on the Rhythm Spacer below equals one quarter note. Observe the amount of space that the quarter note and eighth note use, represented by the shaded areas:

RHYTHM SPACER

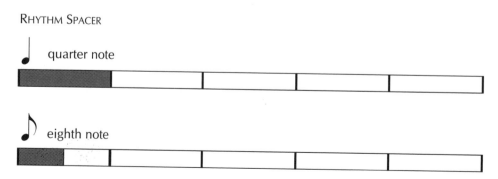

To represent the eighth note on the Rhythm Spacer, it is necessary first to divide the quarter-note box in half with a line, and then to shade one-half of the box.

10 Line up the following groups of notes above the Rhythm Spacer. Draw vertical lines under the eighth notes, and then shade each box to represent the correct values of the quarter and eighth notes. Study the example carefully.

Example

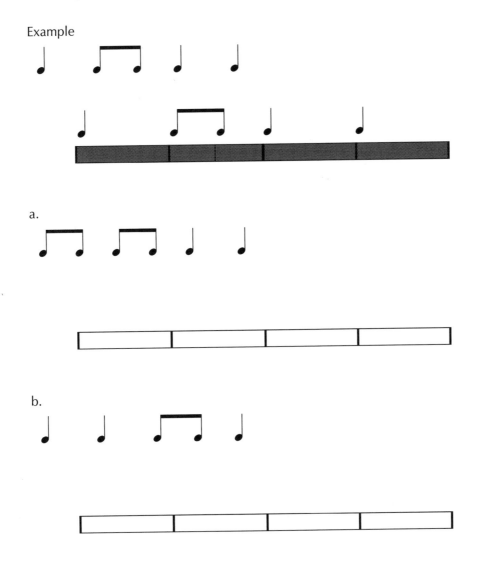

a.

b.

TERMS, SYMBOLS, AND CONCEPTS

rhythm

beat

basic pulse

duration

tempo

♩ quarter note

♪ eighth note

note

notehead

stem

flag

beaming eighth notes

‖: :‖

⌢

notes control space

CHAPTER TWO

Rests

Just as there are symbols that represent musical sounds, there are symbols that represent the absence of musical sound. These are called **rests**. A **quarter rest** (𝄽) has the same time value as a quarter note. In the following rhythms, speak the quarter rest as "rest."

1 Speak with the cassette. Do not clap.

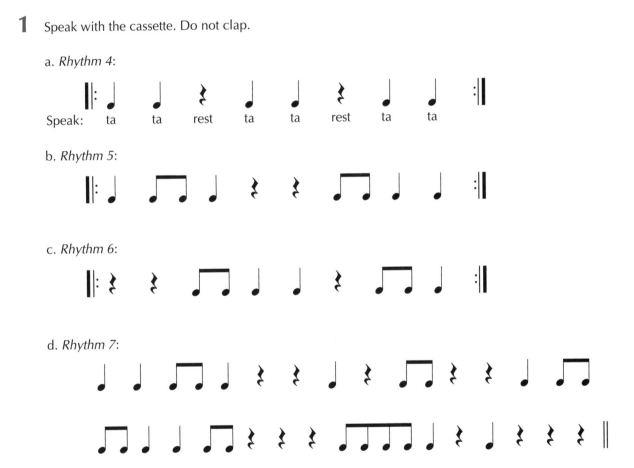

a. *Rhythm 4:*

Speak: ta ta rest ta ta rest ta ta

b. *Rhythm 5:*

c. *Rhythm 6:*

d. *Rhythm 7:*

2 Repeat *Rhythms 4* through *7*. Speak and tap along with the cassette. Do not tap rests; just say "rest," as on the cassette.

3 Repeat these new notations of *Rhythms 4* through *7*. Speak and tap along with the cassette.

a. *Rhythm 4:*

b. *Rhythm 5:*

c. *Rhythm 6:*

d. *Rhythm 7:*

Rests Control Space

Although the quarter rest represents silence, like the quarter note it controls space on the page. The silence has a duration, and when placed on the Rhythm Spacer, the quarter rest takes up one box. To differentiate between a quarter rest and a quarter note on the Rhythm Spacer, we will lightly shade the space that the rest occupies.

4 Place the following rhythms on the Rhythm Spacer. Draw vertical lines under the eighth notes. Use a lighter shading for the rests than for the notes.

a.

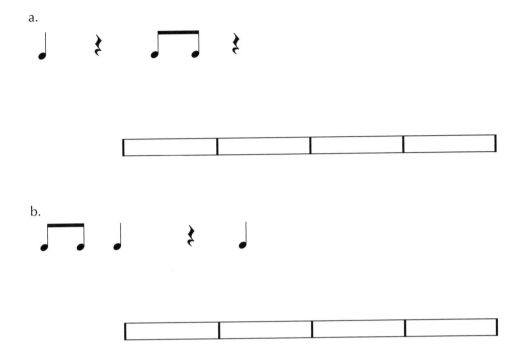

b.

Meter

We naturally hear rhythm in groups of beats. For example, think how often you hear a "tic" followed by a "toc." In music notation, this grouping of beats is called **meter**. Some common groupings are two, three, and four beats. Each group is called a **measure** and is enclosed between two vertical lines, called **bar lines**.

RHYTHMS WITH METER

Strong and Weak Beats

We can often recognize measure divisions when we hear **strong** or **accented** beats followed by **weak** or **unaccented** beats. The first beat of a measure is the strongest. We call this beat the **downbeat**. In the following exercise, the downbeats are indicated by **accent signs** (>).

5 Speak and tap these rhythms. Accent the downbeats by speaking or tapping them a little louder.

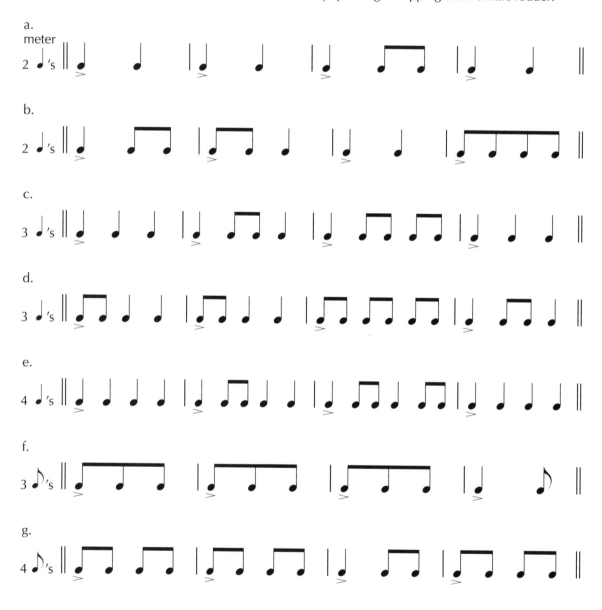

Time Signatures   The meter of a piece is given by a **time signature**, which consists of an upper number indicating how many beats are in each measure, and a lower number indicating which kind of note equals one beat.

6 In the boxes below, write the meaning of the numbers in the indicated signatures, as illustrated above.

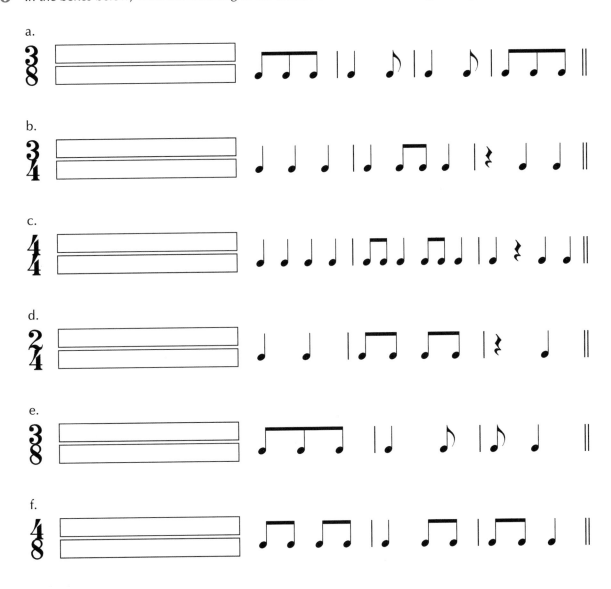

a.

b.

c.

d.

e.

f.

Counting Beats   Speaking the number of each beat in a measure is the most common way of counting. This practice not only provides a steady reference to the basic pulse, it also keeps track of where a rhythm is within a measure.

7   Count each pulse with a steady, even beat:

a.

Count: 1   2   3   1   2   3   1   2   3

b.

Count: 1   2   3   1   2   3   1   2   3

c.

Count: 1   2   3   4   1   2   3   4   1   2   3   4

d.

Count: 1   2   1   2   1   2

Metronome and Tempo   A **metronome** is a mechanical device that supplies a basic pulse at specific tempos. For example, set a metronome at 60, and you will hear 60 even pulses per minute; set it at 100, and you will hear 100 pulses per minute, and so forth. A metronome marking is specified by the letters M.M. with an indication of what kind of note is represented by the basic pulse; for example, M.M. ♩ = 120. A metronome will come in quite handy as you work through the *Rhythm Reader*.

8 Listen to *Rhythms 1–7* on the cassette, and count the meters as indicated.

a. *Rhythm 1:*

Count: 1   2   3   4   1   2   3   4   1   2   3   4   1   2   3   4

b. *Rhythm 2:*

Count: 1   2   3   4   1   2   3   4

c. *Rhythm 3:*

Count: 1   2   3   1   2   3   1   2   3   1   2   3

d. *Rhythm 4:*

Count: 1   2   3   4   1   2   3   4

e. *Rhythm 5:*

Count: 1   2   3   4   1   2   3   4

f. *Rhythm 6:*

Count: 1   2   3   4   1   2   3   4

g. *Rhythm 7:*

Count: 1   2   3   4   1   2   3   4   1   2   3   4   1   2   3   4

Count: 1   2   3   4   1   2   3   4   1   2   3   4

Division of the Basic Pulse

To recite the exact position of notes that are shorter than the basic pulse, we sometimes use the following system of counting. Here, the quarter note represents the basic pulse, and each beat that is divided into eighth notes is given an extra syllable, "and," on the second eighth note.

9 Count with *Rhythms 1–3* on the cassette, dividing the quarter-note beat with "and."

a. *Rhythm 1:*

b. *Rhythm 2:*

c. *Rhythm 3:*

10 Play each of the following exercises on the piano or another keyboard instrument. (If you are using an instrument that does not have a complete range of notes, you may have to play some exercises in the wrong octave.)

a.

TERMS, SYMBOLS, AND CONCEPTS

𝄽

meter
measure
bar line
strong and weak beats

>

time signatures
counting the basic pulse
metronome
dividing the basic pulse

CHAPTER THREE

Eighth Rest

A silence equal in duration to the eighth note (♪) is the **eighth rest** (𝄿). We now know four rhythmic symbols:

quarter note: ♩

quarter rest: 𝄽

eighth note: ♪

eighth rest: 𝄿

Note Values

If the quarter note is the basic pulse, it has a value of one beat. We can then measure other rhythmic symbols against this quarter-note beat.

♩ = 1 beat

𝄽 = 1 beat

♪ = ½ beat

𝄿 = ½ beat

1 Add up the total number of beats in each rhythmic pattern.

Example

♩		𝄽		𝄿		𝄿		♪		♪		♩		♪	= 5 ½ beats
1	+	1	+	½	+	½	+	½	+	½	+	1	+	½	

a.

    𝄽   𝄽   𝄽   𝄽   ♫   =

b.

    𝄿   𝄿   𝄿   𝄿   𝄿   𝄿   𝄿   𝄿   𝄽   =

c.

d.

e.

f.

g.

Speaking the Eighth Rest

When speaking rhythms, say the sound "mm" for the eighth rest. When clapping or tapping a rhythm, speak each rest, but don't clap or tap it. Say "rest" for the quarter rest.

2 Speak these rhythms with the cassette. Do not clap. The count for *Rhythm 11* is "One, two"; the count for *Rhythm 12* is "One, two, three."

a. *Rhythm 8*:

b. *Rhythm 9*:

c. *Rhythm 10*:

d. *Rhythm 11*:

e. *Rhythm 12*:

3 Repeat *Rhythms 8–12*, speaking and clapping. Don't clap the rests, but speak them. Follow the notation in exercise #2, above.

4 Repeat *Rhythms 8–12*. This time count the meter with the rhythms, but do not clap. Divide each quarter-note beat with "and."

a. *Rhythm 8*:

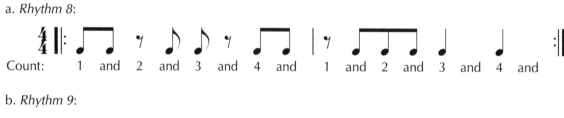

Count: 1   and   2   and   3   and   4   and   1   and   2   and   3   and   4   and

b. *Rhythm 9*:

Count: 1   and   2   and   3   and   4   and   1   and   2   and   3   and   4   and

c. *Rhythm 10*:

Count: 1   and   2   and   3   and   4   and   1   and   2   and   3   and   4   and

d. *Rhythm 11*:

Count: 1   and   2   and   1   and   2   and   1   and   2   and   1   and   2   and

e. *Rhythm 12*:

Count: 1   and   2   and   3   and   1   and   2   and   3   and   1   and   2   and   3   and

5 Count and tap the following rhythms, dividing each quarter-note beat with "and." Before you start tapping, speak a few measures of the count ("one and two and three and four and" for an exercise in $\frac{4}{4}$). When the count feels comfortable, add the tapping. Start with a slow tempo. Remember to keep the count steady.

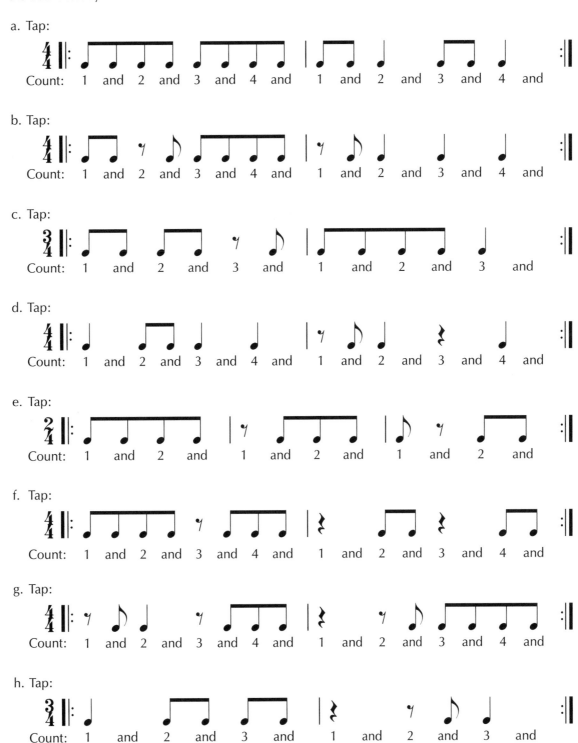

6 Write each of the following rhythms on the Rhythm Spacer. Remember that (1) the eighth rest is equal to the eighth note in duration, and (2) rests are lightly shaded .

a.

b.

c.

d.

e.

1st and 2nd Endings

When an exercise or piece of music contains repeat signs, you may find two endings. If so, when you repeat, skip the measure or measures marked **1st ending** and go directly to the measure or measures marked **2nd ending**.

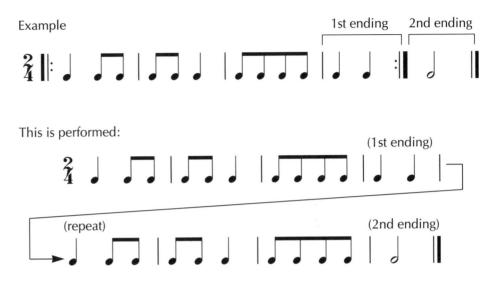

7 Tap the following rhythms.

a.

b.

Other Types of Repeats

D.C. al fine (*da capo al fine*) literally means "from the beginning to the end." If you find this abbreviation at the end of a piece, go back to the beginning and repeat, stopping at the place marked *fine* (end).

D.S. (*dal segno*) literally means "from the sign." If you find the letters *D.S.* at the end of a piece, go back to the sign (𝄋), which is not always at the beginning of the piece but sometimes in the middle, and repeat to the end.

8   Play the following examples.

a.

b.

c.

d.

e.

9   Tap out the rhythms of the following pieces from the *Scorebook.*

  Group Song (*Scorebook* 2)
  Game Song (*Scorebook* 3)
  Brochan Lom (*Scorebook* 6)

TERMS, SYMBOLS, AND CONCEPTS

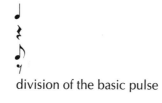

division of the basic pulse

1st and 2nd endings
D.C. al fine
D.S.
𝄋

CHAPTER FOUR

Notes Longer Than the Quarter Note

Most of the rhythms we have studied up until now featured the quarter note as the basic pulse. We will now use the quarter note to measure longer notes.

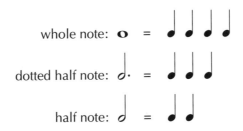

1 Listen to *Rhythms 13–16* on the cassette. The rhythms, notated below, have two parts. The top part is played on a synthesizer, the bottom on a bass drum. The bottom part, which starts the rhythm, gives the quarter-note beat throughout. When you are familiar with each rhythm, tap the top part along with the cassette.

a. *Rhythm 13:*

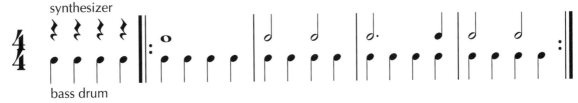

b. *Rhythm 14:*

c. *Rhythm 15:*

d. *Rhythm 16:*

Rests Longer Than the Quarter Rest

Just as different notes represent different durations of musical sound in time, so do different rests represent different durations of silence. The rests that correspond to the whole note, dotted half note, and half note are the following:

whole rest: ▬ = 𝄽 𝄽 𝄽 𝄽

dotted half rest: ▬· = 𝄽 𝄽 𝄽

half rest: ▬ = 𝄽 𝄽

The dotted half rest is used only in the meters that are covered in Chapter Ten ("Different Values of the Basic Pulse") and not in the more common meters of $\frac{2}{4}$, $\frac{3}{4}$, and $\frac{4}{4}$. In $\frac{4}{4}$ meter, we use a half rest followed by a quarter rest to represent three beats of silence.

---

2 Count and tap the following rhythms.

a. Tap:

Count: 1   2   3   4   1   2   3   4   1   2   3   4   1   2   3   4

b. Tap:

Count: 1   2   3   4   1   2   3   4   1   2   3   4   1   2   3   4

c. Tap:

Count: 1   2   3   4   1   2   3   4   1   2   3   4   1   2   3   4

d. Tap:

Count: 1   2   3   4   1   2   3   4   1   2   3   4   1   2   3   4

Anacrusis

Sometimes a piece of music begins in the middle or last part of a measure, before the first downbeat. This partial opening measure is called an **anacrusis** (occasionally a **pickup** or **upbeat**). The value of the anacrusis is *subtracted from the last measure of the piece.* Observe the anacrusis in the following examples:

Counting the Anacrusis

There are two ways a performer can count the meter of a piece that begins with an anacrusis. First, it is important to recognize the relationship of the opening note or notes to the meter:

1.

2.

One way to prepare the downbeat is to count an entire measure and fit the opening notes where they belong at the end of a measure:

1.

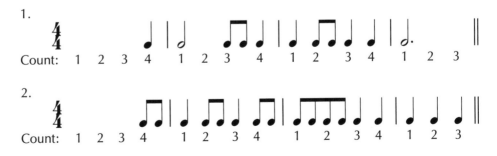

Count: 1   2   3   4   1   2   3   4   1   2   3   4   1   2   3

2.

Count: 1   2   3   4   1   2   3   4   1   2   3   4   1   2   3

Another way is to "pick up" the count some time after "1" of this imaginary measure, thereby establishing the meter without counting out an entire measure:

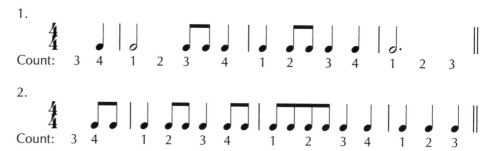

3   Each of the following rhythms contains an anacrusis. Position the notes correctly above the counted numbers. Draw the bar lines *through* the numbers. Tap each rhythm when it is complete. Study the example carefully.

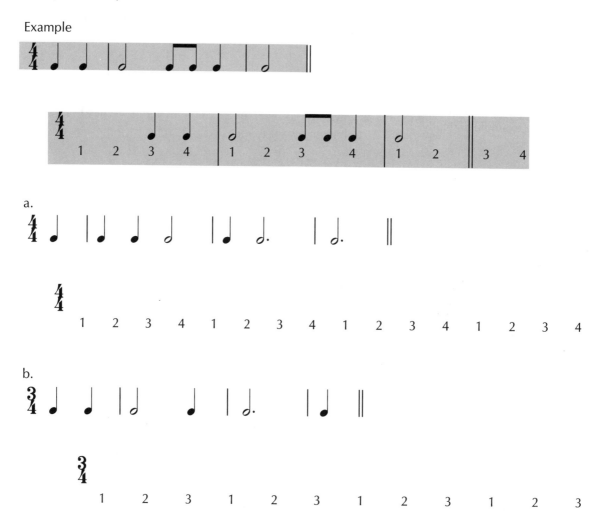

c.

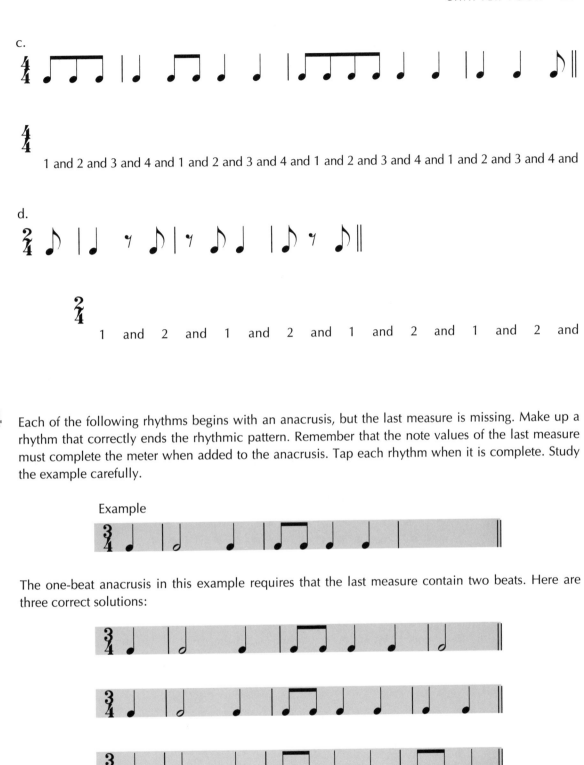

4/4

1 and 2 and 3 and 4 and 1 and 2 and 3 and 4 and 1 and 2 and 3 and 4 and 1 and 2 and 3 and 4 and

d.

2/4

1   and   2   and   1   and   2   and   1   and   2   and   1   and   2   and

4 Each of the following rhythms begins with an anacrusis, but the last measure is missing. Make up a rhythm that correctly ends the rhythmic pattern. Remember that the note values of the last measure must complete the meter when added to the anacrusis. Tap each rhythm when it is complete. Study the example carefully.

Example

The one-beat anacrusis in this example requires that the last measure contain two beats. Here are three correct solutions:

a.

b.

c.

d.

e.

f.

g.

h.

5 Listen to *Rhythms 17–20* on the cassette. Notice that the lower part in the rhythmic patterns below provides the basic pulse. When you are familiar with the rhythms, tap the top part along with the recording. Repeat several times.

a. *Rhythm 17*:

b. *Rhythm 18*:

c. *Rhythm 19*:

d. *Rhythm 20*:

Conducting   The basic conducting patterns are given below. By performing them, you will translate each meter into physical action. The lines indicate the motion of the arm led by the hand. The motion should be free and flowing. As you develop the basic movements, count the meter.

6 Play these basic conducting patterns. Start at the asterisk.

2 basic pulses

($\frac{2}{2}$ or $\frac{2}{4}$)

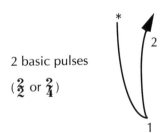

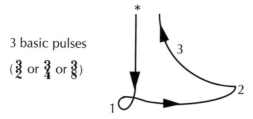

3 basic pulses

($\frac{3}{2}$ or $\frac{3}{4}$ or $\frac{3}{8}$)

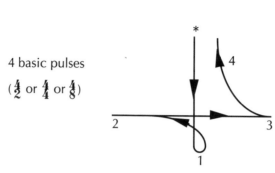

4 basic pulses

($\frac{4}{2}$ or $\frac{4}{4}$ or $\frac{4}{8}$)

7 Play the following.

a.

b.

c.

d.

e.

8 Tap out the following pieces from the *Scorebook*:

Lullaby (Apache) (*Scorebook* 1)
Fray Diego (*Scorebook* 4)
O du schöner Rosengarten (*Scorebook* 5)
Oliver and the Maiden (*Scorebook* 7)
Philis, plus avare que tendre (*Scorebook* 8)
Die Gedanken sind frei (*Scorebook* 9)
Oh How Lovely Is the Evening (*Scorebook* 44)

TERMS, SYMBOLS, AND CONCEPTS

anacrusis
conducting patterns

CHAPTER FIVE

Note System

In the Western notation system, the whole note may be divided into smaller notes. The symbol for each note and its equivalent rest is presented below. The duration of each note or rest in this list is *half the duration* of the note or rest above it.

Note Name	Note Symbol	Rest Symbol
whole note		
half note		
quarter note		
eighth note		
sixteenth note		
thirty-second note		
sixty-fourth note		

Beams

Notes smaller than the quarter note are written with flags (♪ ♪ ♪). When a group of flagged notes are written together, unifying beams are used.

Notice that the number of flags is replaced by the same number of beams.

Combinations of Notes with Beams

Notes of different time values can be joined together with beams when they all occur within the same beat.

The beam may be on the left or right side of the note stem. It is the number of beams that touch the stem that determines the value of the note.

1 Rewrite these rhythms with flags.

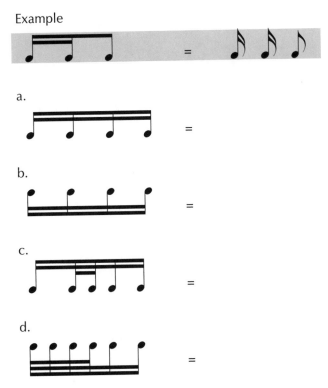

Example

a.

b.

c.

d.

Relationship of Note Values

The quarter note is often used as the basic unit for measuring the values of other notes. Below, each note is expressed in quarter notes.

1. Notes larger than the quarter note:

$$\mathbf{o} \;=\; \text{♩ ♩ ♩ ♩}$$

$$\text{𝅗𝅥.} \;=\; \text{♩ ♩ ♩}$$

$$\text{𝅗𝅥} \;=\; \text{♩ ♩}$$

2. Notes smaller than the quarter note are often beamed in groups equal to one quarter note in duration:

---

2 Write the number of smaller-value notes that equal the indicated larger-value note.

Example

$$\mathbf{o} = \left(\text{in } \text{𝅗𝅥} \right) \quad \text{𝅗𝅥} \quad \text{𝅗𝅥}$$

a.

$$\text{𝅗𝅥.} = \left(\text{in } \text{♩} \right)$$

b.

$$\text{𝅗𝅥} = \left(\text{in } \text{♩} \right)$$

c.

$$\text{♩} = \left(\text{in } \text{♪} \right)$$

d.

$$\text{𝅗𝅥} = \left(\text{in } \text{♪} \right)$$

e.

$$\mathbf{o} = \left(\text{in } \text{♪} \right)$$

f.

$\mathbf{J} = \left(_{in} \, \mathbf{\Lambda} \right)$

g.

$\mathbf{\rho}^{\cdot} = \left(_{in} \, \mathbf{\rho} \right)$

h.

$\mathbf{\rho}^{\cdot} = \left(_{in} \, \mathbf{\beta} \right)$

i.

$\mathbf{\rho} = \left(_{in} \, \mathbf{\rho} \right)$

The Tie

Two notes of the same pitch may be connected with a curved line joining one notehead to the other. This line is called a **tie**. The first note is then prolonged by the value of the second. (The second is not played.)

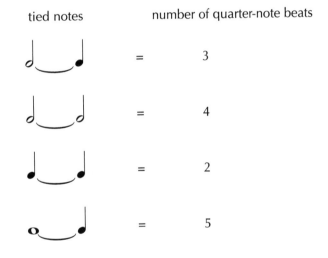

tied notes		number of quarter-note beats
	=	3
	=	4
	=	2
	=	5

Do not confuse the tie with a similar curved line called the **slur**, which indicates that two or more *different* pitches are to be played smoothly (see *Workbook*, Appendixes I, X). The tie always joins two notes of the same pitch.

The Dotted Note   We have already learned about one dotted note, the dotted half note (𝅗𝅥.). But any note can be dotted. A dot after a note lengthens the note by half its own value. Notice that prolonging a note with the addition of a dot is an alternative to using a tie to accomplish the same purpose.

The dot is *always* placed in a space, even when the note it augments falls on a line. For example:

3   With the quarter note valued at one beat, give the numerical value of each of these notes or groups of notes.

Examples

a. =

b. =

c. =

d. =

e. =

f. =

g. =

h. =

i. =

j. =

4 Write one note that equals each of these rhythmic groupings.

Example

a. =

b. =

c. =

d. =

e. =

f. =

g. =

h. =

i. =

5 Name each symbol and give its value, with the quarter note valued at one beat.

6 Give the total of each rhythmic group, with the quarter note valued at one beat.

Example

$$ = 3 $$

a.

$= $

c.

$ = $

b.

$ = $

d.

$ = $

Rests

When writing rests, musicians follow certain practices that differ from the way notes are written.

1. The whole rest (▬) may represent a full measure of rest *in any meter*. It always hangs beneath the *fourth* line of the staff in the *center* of the measure.

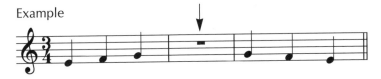

Example

2. Rests are not tied.
3. Half rests (▬) always sit atop the third line. They are rarely used in $\frac{3}{4}$.
4. Quarter rests (𝄽) and half rests (▬) are usually written on the beat, not in between the beats.

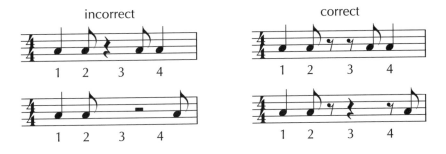

7   Play the following exercises.

a.

b.

c.

TERMS, SYMBOLS, AND CONCEPTS

o ▬		beam
♩ ▬		flag
♩ 𝄽		tie
♪ 𝄾		slur
♫ 𝄿		dotted note
♬ 𝅀		
♬ 𝅁		

CHAPTER SIX

Working with Ties and Dotted Notes

Rhythms that feature tied or dotted notes require special attention when related to the basic pulse. Observe the positions of the following tied or dotted notes on the Rhythm Spacer:

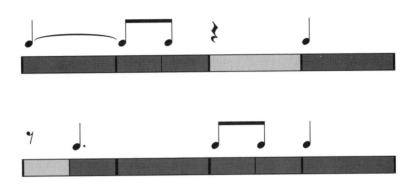

---

1 Write each of the following rhythms on the provided Rhythm Spacer.

a.

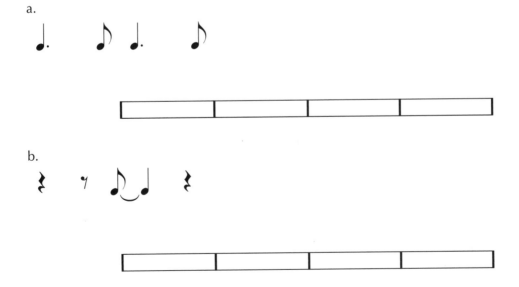

b.

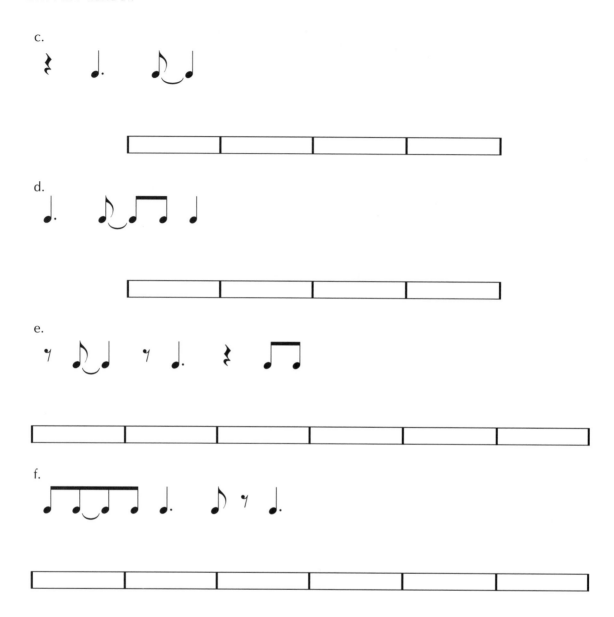

c.

d.

e.

f.

2 Listen to *Rhythms 21–23* on the cassette. Notice that the lower notated part provides the basic pulse. When you are familiar with the rhythms, tap the top part along with the recording.

a. *Rhythm 21:*

b. *Rhythm 22*:

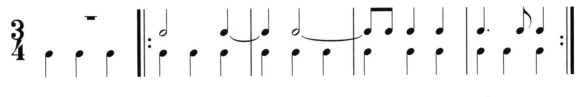

c. *Rhythm 23*:

Division of the Basic Pulse

Counting the basic pulse with the "one and two and" method can help you understand how to perform tied or dotted rhythms. Observe the division of the basic pulse in the following examples:

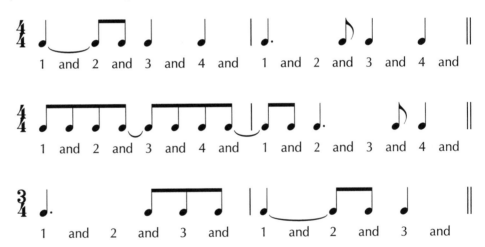

3 Position each of the following rhythms above the divided pulse, as in the examples above. Tap each rhythm as you count it.

a.

Coordinating Both Hands

Until now, we have tapped and counted one part at a time. Now we will begin tapping two parts simultaneously. Not only will this process help you understand certain rhythms, it will also help to give you the coordination necessary to play many musical instruments.

4 Tap the following rhythms separately.

a. Use the right hand:

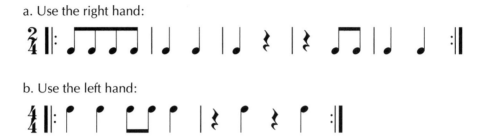

b. Use the left hand:

5 a. Now tap with both hands at once. Tap eighth notes with the right hand against quarters with the left:

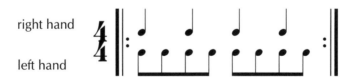

b. Repeat with the parts reversed:

6 Tap these rhythms. First start the left hand *alone.* When you have established the basic pulse, *add* the right hand.

a. Speak and tap:

b.

right hand

left hand

c.

right hand

left hand

d.

right hand

left hand

7   Tap *Rhythms 13–16* with the cassette, using both hands.

a. *Rhythm 13*:

synthesizer

bass drum

b. *Rhythm 14*:

c. *Rhythm 15*:

d. *Rhythm 16*:

8 Tap the following rhythms using both hands.

a.

right hand

left hand

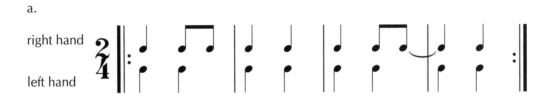

b.

right hand

left hand

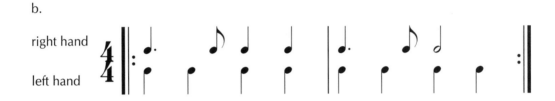

c.

right hand

left hand

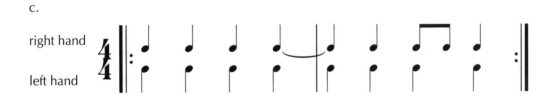

d.

right hand

left hand

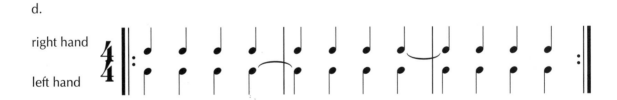

e.

right hand

left hand

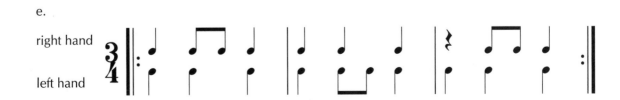

9   Play these exercises.

a.

b.

c.

10   Tap the rhythms from the following *Scorebook* pieces:

Cradle Song (*Scorebook* 13)
O'er the Burn, Bessie (*Scorebook* 17)
The Hunter (*Scorebook* 18)
Oh Freedom (*Scorebook* 39)
Dona nobis pacem (*Scorebook* 43)
Beethoven, *Ode to Joy* (*Scorebook* 59)
Mozart, Theme from *Don Giovanni* (*Scorebook* 60)
Morley, *Nancie* (*Scorebook* 61)

TERMS, SYMBOLS, AND CONCEPTS

counting ties and dotted notes
two-hand coordination

CHAPTER SEVEN

Subdivision of the Quarter Note into Sixteenth Notes

The quarter note can be subdivided into four parts with the use of sixteenth notes. The symbol for a sixteenth note is a 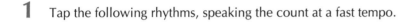. Notice that it has two flags (or two beams) on its stem. When speaking the following patterns, accent "one" in each group of four.

1 Tap the following rhythms, speaking the count at a fast tempo.

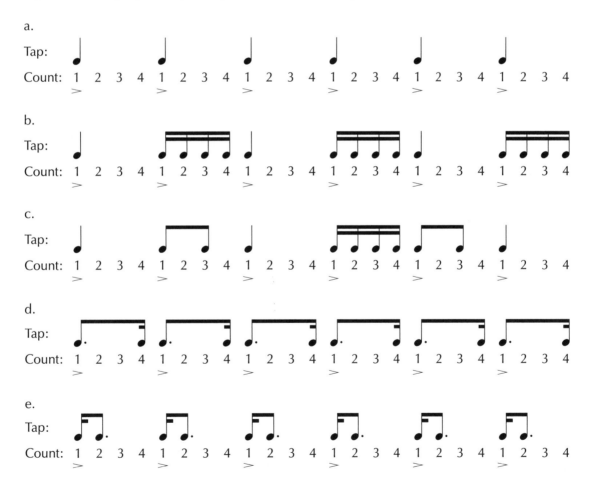

f.

Tap:

Count:
1 2 3 4   1 2 3 4   1 2 3 4   1 2 3 4   1 2 3 4   1 2 3 4
>   >   >   >   >   >

g.

Tap:

Count:
1 2 3 4   1 2 3 4   1 2 3 4   1 2 3 4   1 2 3 4   1 2 3 4
>   >   >   >   >   >

h.

Tap:

Count:
1 2 3 4   1 2 3 4   1 2 3 4   1 2 3 4   1 2 3 4   1 2 3 4
>   >   >   >   >   >

2 Rewrite the rhythms found in exercise #1 below the subdivisions. Write the stems down.

a.
>   >   >   >   >   >
1 2 3 4   1 2 3 4   1 2 3 4   1 2 3 4   1 2 3 4   1 2 3 4

b.
>   >   >   >   >   >
1 2 3 4   1 2 3 4   1 2 3 4   1 2 3 4   1 2 3 4   1 2 3 4

c.
>   >   >   >   >   >
1 2 3 4   1 2 3 4   1 2 3 4   1 2 3 4   1 2 3 4   1 2 3 4

d.
>   >   >   >   >   >
1 2 3 4   1 2 3 4   1 2 3 4   1 2 3 4   1 2 3 4   1 2 3 4

e.
>   >   >   >   >   >
1 2 3 4   1 2 3 4   1 2 3 4   1 2 3 4   1 2 3 4   1 2 3 4

f.

>   >   >   >   >   >

1 2 3 4 1 2 3 4 1 2 3 4 1 2 3 4 1 2 3 4 1 2 3 4

g.

>   >   >   >   >   >

1 2 3 4 1 2 3 4 1 2 3 4 1 2 3 4 1 2 3 4 1 2 3 4

h.

>   >   >   >   >   >

1 2 3 4 1 2 3 4 1 2 3 4 1 2 3 4 1 2 3 4 1 2 3 4

Speaking Sixteenth Notes in Meter

When subdividing into sixteenth notes within a metered rhythm that uses the quarter note as the basic beat, the sixteenth notes can be counted in this way: "one ee and a" (spoken slurred together, with the accent on "one").

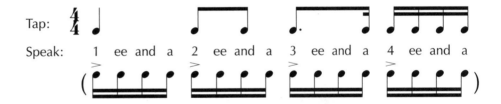

This method helps you keep track of the beat within the measure while still subdividing each beat into four parts.

3 Tap and speak as indicated.

a.

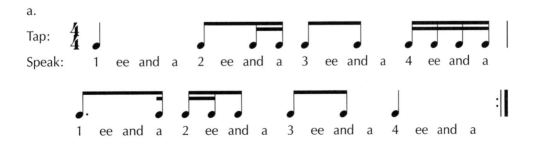

b.

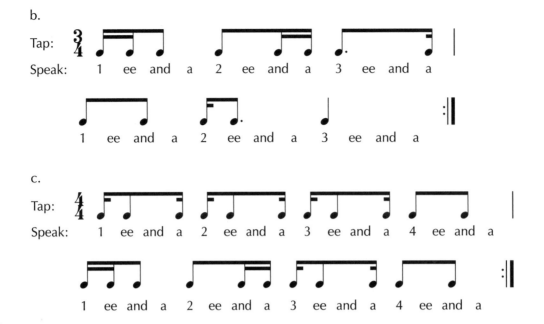

Tap: $\frac{3}{4}$

Speak: 1   ee   and   a   2   ee   and   a   3   ee   and   a

         1   ee   and   a   2   ee   and   a   3   ee   and   a

c.

Tap: $\frac{4}{4}$

Speak: 1   ee   and   a   2   ee   and   a   3   ee   and   a   4   ee   and   a

         1   ee   and   a   2   ee   and   a   3   ee   and   a   4   ee   and   a

4   Tap with your right hand and count. The pulse equals the quarter note.

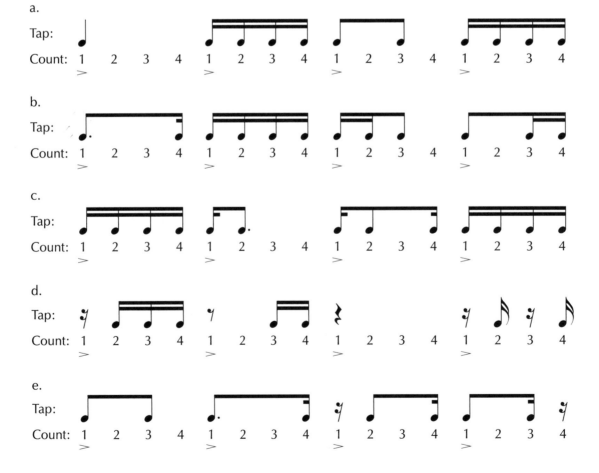

a.

Tap:

Count: 1   2   3   4   1   2   3   4   1   2   3   4   1   2   3   4

b.

Tap:

Count: 1   2   3   4   1   2   3   4   1   2   3   4   1   2   3   4

c.

Tap:

Count: 1   2   3   4   1   2   3   4   1   2   3   4   1   2   3   4

d.

Tap:

Count: 1   2   3   4   1   2   3   4   1   2   3   4   1   2   3   4

e.

Tap:

Count: 1   2   3   4   1   2   3   4   1   2   3   4   1   2   3   4

f.

5   Write each of the rhythms in exercise #4 above the divided pulse. Tap each rhythm with the spoken count.

e.

1   ee   and   a   2   ee   and   a   3   ee   and   a   4   ee   and   a

f.

1   ee   and   a   2   ee   and   a   3   ee   and   a   4   ee   and   a

6   Tap with both hands.

a.

right hand

left hand

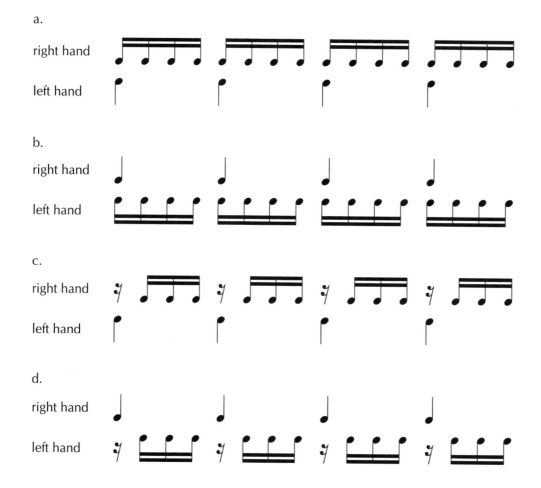

b.

right hand

left hand

c.

right hand

left hand

d.

right hand

left hand

e.

right hand

left hand

f.

right hand

left hand

7 Tap and count the following exercises.

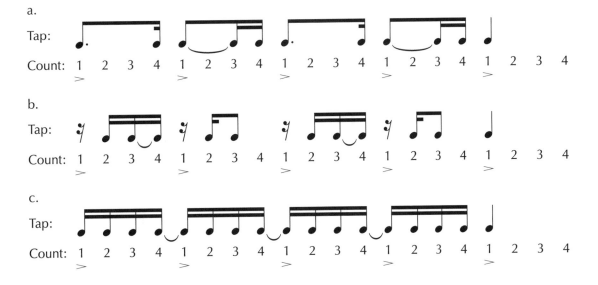

a.

Tap:

Count: 1   2   3   4   1   2   3   4   1   2   3   4   1   2   3   4   1   2   3   4

b.

Tap:

Count: 1   2   3   4   1   2   3   4   1   2   3   4   1   2   3   4   1   2   3   4

c.

Tap:

Count: 1   2   3   4   1   2   3   4   1   2   3   4   1   2   3   4   1   2   3   4

8 Listen to *Rhythms 24–29* on the cassette. Repeat, tapping the left-hand part only to get a sense of each rhythm. Repeat, tapping the right-hand part only. You may wish to work up to tapping both parts simultaneously. On the recording, the rhythms are grouped *24–26* and *27–29*.

a. *Rhythm 24:*

right hand

left hand

b. *Rhythm 25*:

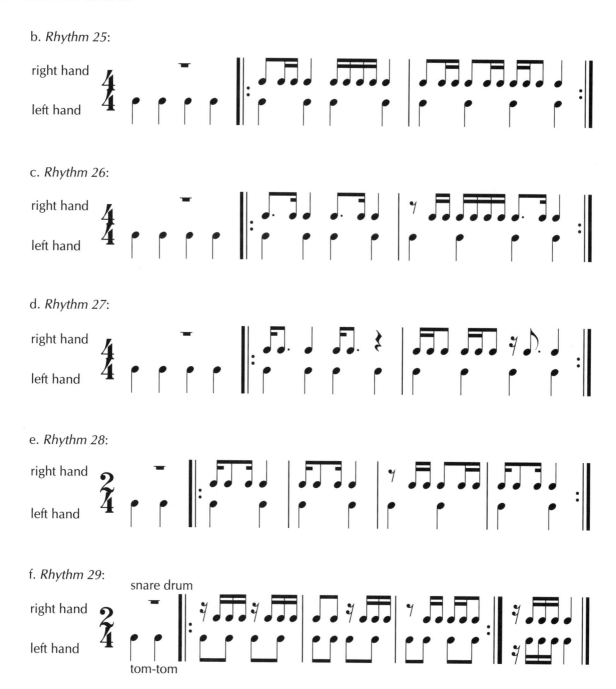

c. *Rhythm 26*:

d. *Rhythm 27*:

e. *Rhythm 28*:

f. *Rhythm 29*:

Aligning Two Parts   Notes that sound together are written directly above or below each other. The correct spacing of two separate parts shows exactly where the notes occur. In the following exercises, it is no longer necessary to shade parts of the Rhythm Spacer. Simply divide the beat with a line to indicate where a note is played. Study the example carefully.

Example

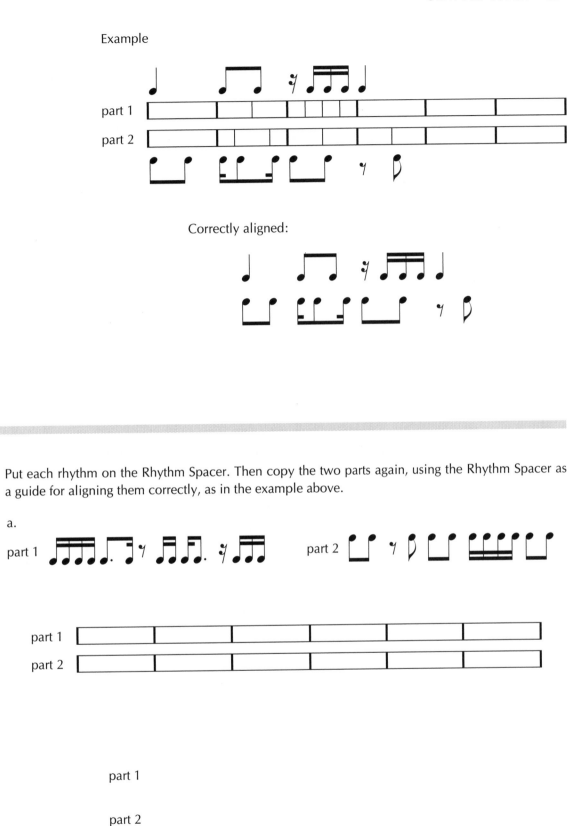

Correctly aligned:

9 Put each rhythm on the Rhythm Spacer. Then copy the two parts again, using the Rhythm Spacer as a guide for aligning them correctly, as in the example above.

a.

part 1

part 2

part 1

part 2

b.

part 1 ♫ ♫ ♫ ♫ ♪ ♪ ♪ ♪ ♫ part 2

part 1

part 2

part 1

part 2

Marking the Beat

The Rhythm Spacer is a good tool to use when you want to highlight where beats and parts of a beat occur. In real musical practice, however, it would prove too cumbersome to use. Musicians often create a shorthand version by drawing lines where the beats occur.

rhythm

quarter-note beat   /   /   /   /   /   /

These lines serve to locate the beat much like the Rhythm Spacer does.

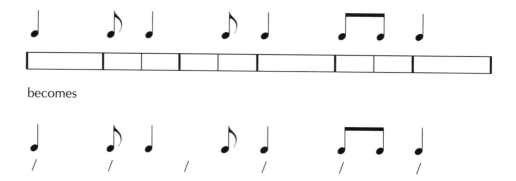

becomes

10 Mark where the quarter-note beat falls. You can follow this procedure whether or not the rhythm has a meter sign.

Example

a.

b.

c.

d.

e.

11 Play these exercises.

a.

12 Tap the following pieces from the *Scorebook.*

Jeune fillete (*Scorebook* 16)
Carraig Aonair (*Scorebook* 19)
The Knife Sharpener (*Scorebook* 21)
Hymn (Armenian) (*Scorebook* 22)
The Oak and the Ash (*Scorebook* 35)
Rossini, *Cujus animam* (*Scorebook* 71)

TERMS, SYMBOLS, AND CONCEPTS

subdivision of the quarter note   aligning two parts
counting sixteenths   marking the beat

CHAPTER EIGHT

Simple and Compound Meters

All of the meters we have studied so far feature a basic pulse that is divided into two; such a meter is called a **simple meter**. There are also meters whose basic pulse regularly divides into three parts; such a meter is called a **compound meter**.

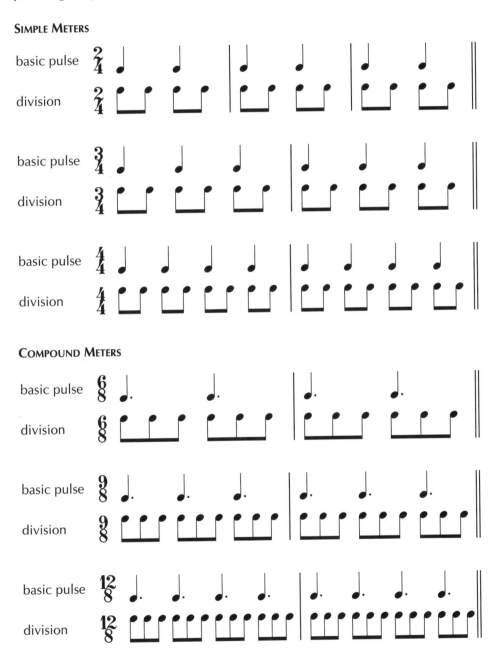

Counting Compound Meter

The simple meters we have encountered have used the quarter note as the basic pulse. With compound meters, the dotted quarter note is most often the basic pulse. Methods for counting compound meters vary depending upon which meter is being counted and at what tempo. For example, $\frac{6}{8}$, the most common coupound meter, can be counted in the following ways:

Ways to Count $\frac{6}{8}$

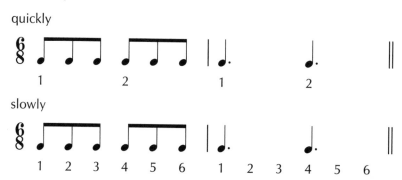

quickly

slowly

The first example emphasizes the basic pulse and is used for moderate to quick tempos. The second emphasizes the eighth-note divisions of the basic pulse (which is what the time signature indicates to us) and is used mainly for slow tempos.

1 Tap and count these rhythms.

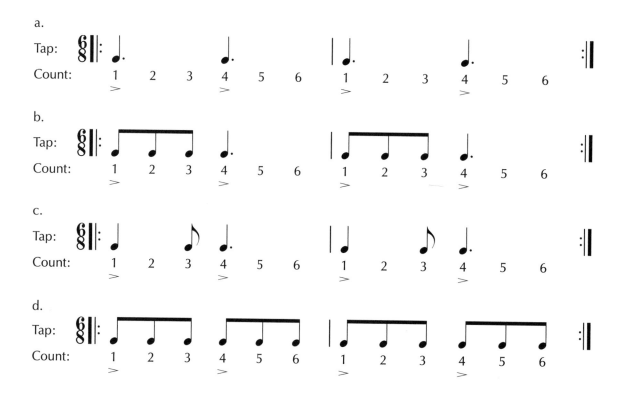

e.

2 Tap and count these rhythms. First tap the left hand. Add the counting. Then add the right hand.

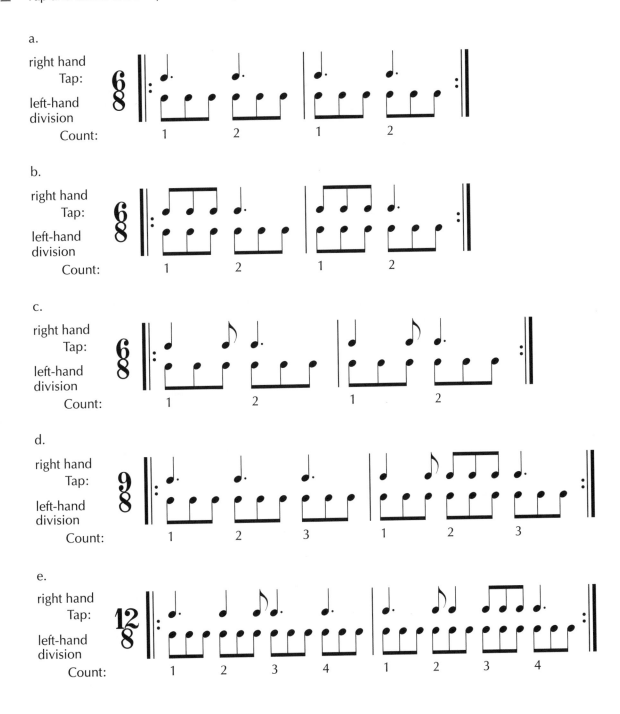

3 Follow the score of *Greensleeves* (*Scorebook* 33) as you listen to it on the cassette. Count the melody in two different ways: count the subdivisions (♪♪♪ ♪♪♪), and count the basic pulse (♩. ♩.). After

  1 2 3 4 5 6   1 2

listening and counting a few times, tap the melody while following the score.

4 Tap the first rhythmic figure of *Silent Night* with your right hand against even eighth notes tapped with your left. Singing it will help. Repeat until you have the rhythm right.

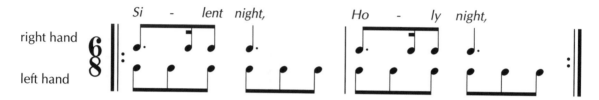

5 Now tap out the entire melody of *Silent Night* (*Scorebook* 38), using your right hand for the melody and your left hand for the division of the beat.

6 Listen to *Rhythms 30–32*. After you are familiar with the rhythmic structure, tap out the parts separately, then together. Repeat, counting the meter.

a. *Rhythm 30*:

b. *Rhythm 31*:

c. *Rhythm 32*:

Speaking Compound Meter

If you want to count aloud in compound meter and indicate both the basic pulse and its subdivision, you can do it this way:

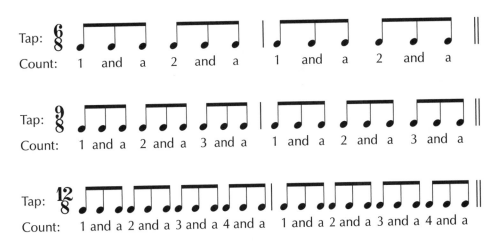

7 Tap and count the following rhythms using the "one and a two and a" method.

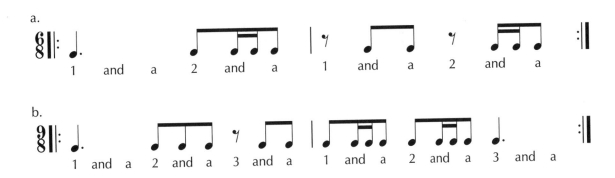

c.

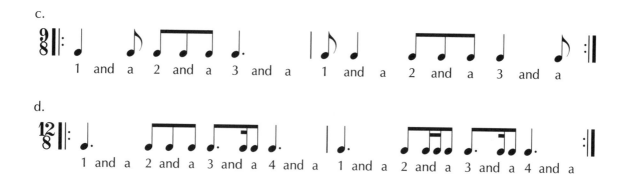

d.

8   Play these exercises.

a.

b.

c.

9   Tap the following pieces from the *Scorebook*.

Drink to Me Only with Thine Eyes (*Scorebook* 28)
Believe Me if All Those Endearing Young Charms (*Scorebook* 42)
Haydn, Theme from *Symphony No. 100* (*Scorebook* 68)

TERMS, SYMBOLS, AND CONCEPTS

simple meter
compound meter

basic pulse in compound meter
counting in compound meters

CHAPTER NINE

Triplets

Any note can be divided into three equal parts. Such a division is called a **triplet**. In this chapter, we will consider the triplet division of the quarter note, which is notated . Notice how the triplets line up with quarter notes.

1 Tap *Rhythm 33* with the cassette. The top part is played by a snare drum, the bottom part by a bass drum.

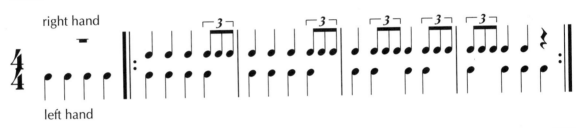

right hand

left hand

Triplets and Eighth Notes

The use of triplets in a simple meter such as $\frac{4}{4}$ allows the quarter note to be divided into three parts as well as two. It is essential to understand the relationship between the normal eighth note and the triplet made out of eighth notes. This difference between the two is demonstrated on the Rhythm Spacer below.

Observe how triplets are aligned on the Rhythm Spacer:

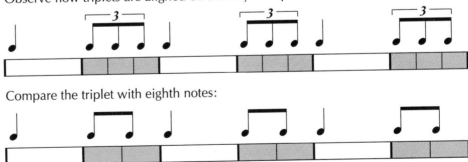

Compare the triplet with eighth notes:

Notice that only the use of a bracket and the number 3 (⌐3⌐) distinguishes eighth notes from triplets.

2 Align each pair of rhythms on the Rhythm Spacer, as indicated. You need not use shading.

a.

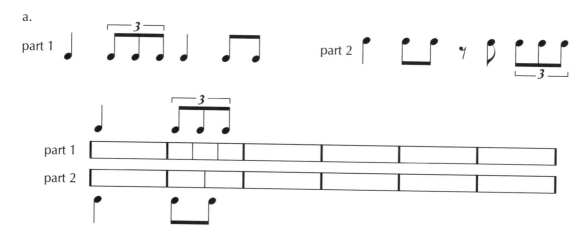

b.

c.

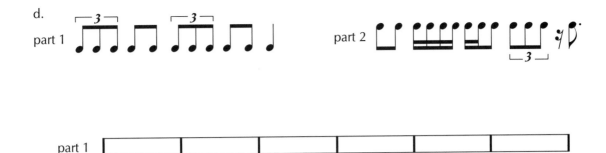

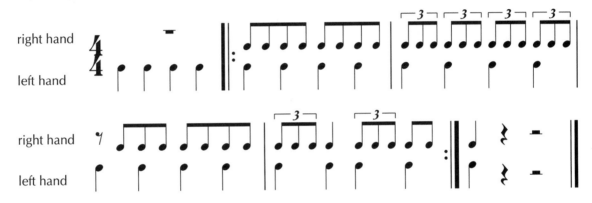

3 Tap both parts of *Rhythm 34*. Listen to the difference between eighth notes and triplets.

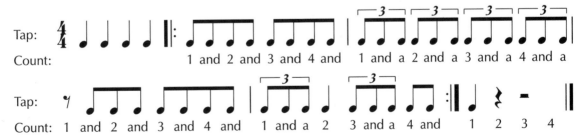

Speaking Triplets   The quarter note is divided into *two* equal parts by counting "one and two and." The quarter note can be divided into *three* equal parts by counting "one and a two and a three and a four and a."

---

4 Tap and count the top part of *Rhythm 34*.

Tap: 4/4 𝅘𝅥 𝅘𝅥 𝅘𝅥 𝅘𝅥 ‖: ♫ ♫ ♫ ♫ | ♪♪♪ ♪♪♪ ♪♪♪ ♪♪♪ |
Count: 1 and 2 and 3 and 4 and   1 and a 2 and a 3 and a 4 and a

Tap: ♪ ♫ ♫ ♫ ♫ | ♪♪♪ 𝅘𝅥 ♪♪♪ ♫ :‖ 𝅘𝅥 𝄽 — ‖
Count: 1 and 2 and 3 and 4 and   1 and a 2   3 and a 4 and   1   2   3   4

The Triplet Rest   When a rest occurs within a triplet, it is written like the eighth rest, but included within the triplet bracket.

5   Tap and count the following exercises.

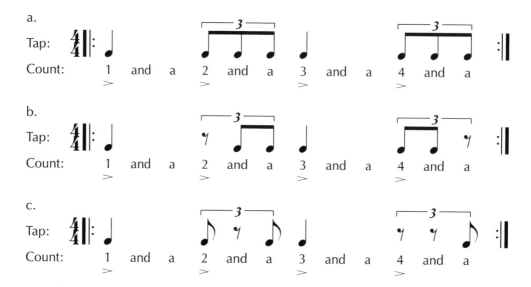

6   Tap the top part of *Rhythm 35* with the cassette. Then tap the bottom part.

The Triplet and the Basic Pulse

In Chapter Eight, we learned how to count three eighth notes per beat in compound meter. There is an important difference between these eighth notes and the triplets discussed above. The difference lies in the basic pulse. If the meter is compound and the basic pulse is a dotted quarter, a natural three-eighths division occurs without special notation. However, when the basic pulse is a quarter note, the triplet bracket is needed in order to signify a three-part division.

Compare:

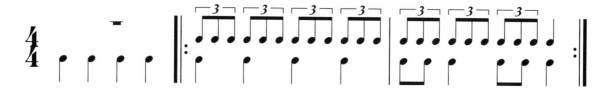

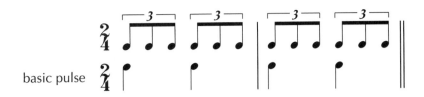

basic pulse

---

7 Play these exercises.

a.

b.

c.

8 Tap the following pieces from the *Scorebook.*

La paloma (*Scorebook* 36)
Mozart, *Minuet* (top part only) (*Scorebook* 73)

TERMS, SYMBOLS, AND CONCEPTS

┌─ *3* ─┐
triple rest

triplet and the basic pulse

CHAPTER TEN

Different Values of the Basic Pulse

In the rhythms studied so far, the basic pulse has been ♩ or ♩. . Other note values can represent the basic pulse, depending on the tempo, the historical period in which a piece was composed, or the intention of the composer. Observe these examples:

FOUR BEATS TO THE MEASURE

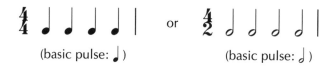

THREE BEATS TO THE MEASURE

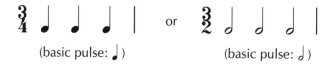

TWO BEATS TO THE MEASURE

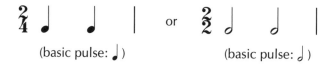

TWO BEATS TO THE MEASURE

C and ¢

The symbol **C** represents common time, or $\frac{4}{4}$. The fact that it's called common time indicates the frequency with which this time signature is used. The symbol **¢** (the *alla breve* sign) is equal to $\frac{2}{2}$ meter and indicates that the basic number of beats per measure is halved, while the unit of pulse is doubled.

You can make the ratio of note values smaller as well as larger, as illustrated by this example:

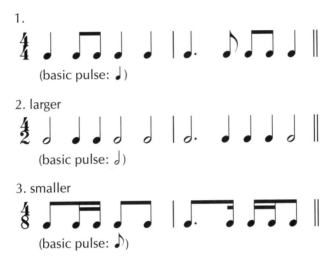

All three rhythms sound exactly alike, if the tempo of the basic pulse is the same. Notice that example 2 is created by doubling the original quarter-note pulse, while example 3 divides the original quarter-note pulse in half.

Double Whole Note and Rest

Rhythms that use the half note as the basic pulse and have four beats per measure may require the use of a **double whole note** or its equivalent rest, the **double whole rest**. The double whole rest, used in $\frac{4}{2}$, is the only exception to the rule of using the normal whole rest (▬) to indicate a measure of silence in any meter. The values of this note and rest are:

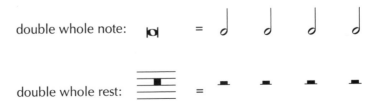

1 Tap *Rhythm 13* with the cassette, first in its original form, then in the other two versions. Study the relationship among the three examples.

a.

b.

c.

2 Tap *Rhythm 17* with the cassette, first in its original form, then in the other two versions. Study the relationship among the three examples.

a.

b.

c.

3 Write the following rhythms two other ways, as in the exercises above. Double the value of the basic pulse, then halve it.

a.

4 Tap these three versions of *Rhythm 33* with the cassette.

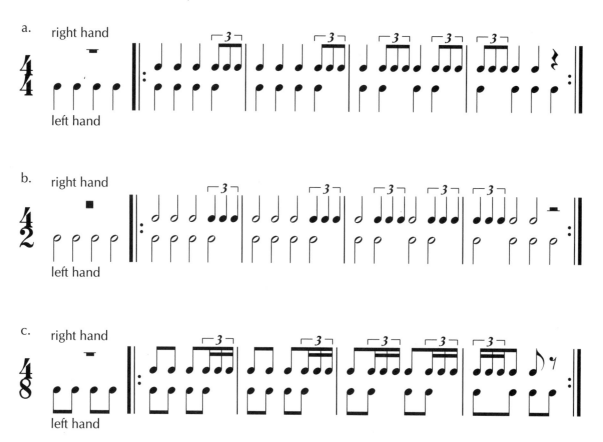

Triplets with Different Note Values

Triplets can be written with any note value. Unlike notes that are divided into two parts, triplets require a bracket and the number 3 to show that the beat is divided into three parts. Compare the following:

divided by 2

divided by 3

5 Write the following rhythm two ways. First double, then halve the value.

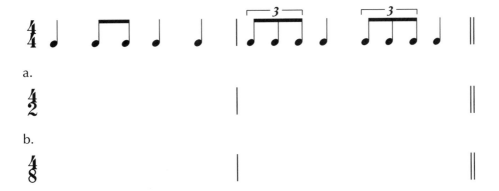

a.

b.

6 Tap out the rhythm of *Greensleeves* (Cassette) along with the recording. Follow the original version (a) for the first verse. Follow the alternative notation (b) for the second verse.

7   Rewrite each of these rhythms in a different meter, as indicated.

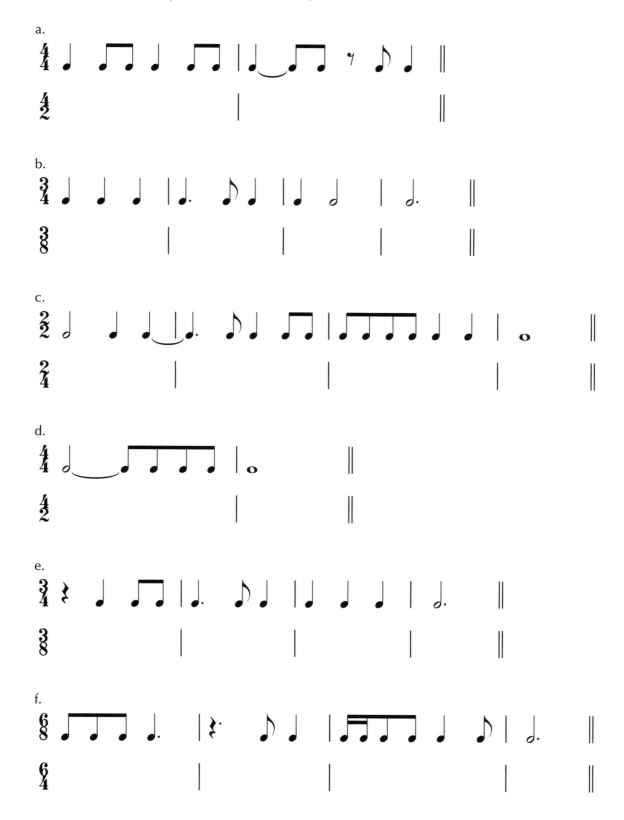

8 Play or tap the following melodies.

a.

b.

9 Tap the following pieces from the *Scorebook.*

Dream Song (*Scorebook* 24)
Christmas Has Come (*Scorebook* 51)
Byrd, *Galiarda* (*Scorebook* 62)

TERMS, SYMBOLS, AND CONCEPTS

using different note values for the
   basic pulse
𝄴 and 𝄵
doubling the value of the basic
   pulse

dividing the value of the basic
   pulse

triplets with different note values

CHAPTER ELEVEN

Syncopation

We have concentrated thus far on rhythms whose accented notes fall *on* the beat. When accented notes fall *between* beats or *off* the beat, they create **syncopated** rhythms. The fastest way to learn syncopated rhythms is to speak them. In the following exercise, use the speaking system that we learned in Chapter One.

1   Speak *Rhythms 36–38* with the cassette.

a. *Rhythm 36*:

b. *Rhythm 37*:

c. *Rhythm 38*:

Syncopated and Nonsyncopated Rhythms

Notes can occur *on* or *off* the beat. When the note that represents the basic pulse occurs off the beat, the duration of that note extends into the next beat. This phenomenon creates a syncopated rhythmic pattern:

on the beat (nonsyncopated)

off the beat (syncopated)

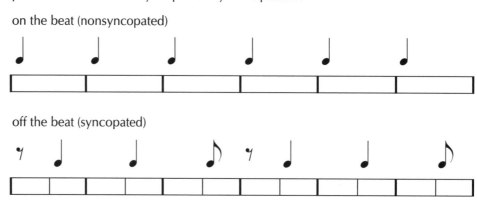

2 Line up the following syncopated rhythms on the Rhythm Spacer.

a.

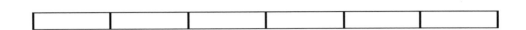

b.

c.

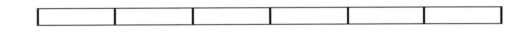

d.

e.

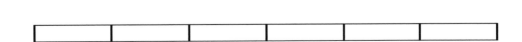

f.

3   In the syncopated rhythms below, mark where the quarter-note beat falls.

a.

b.

c.

4   Rewrite *Rhythms 36–38* (exercise #1), aligning them with a quarter-note pulse. Tap both parts. Do not speak.

a. *Rhythm 36:*

b. *Rhythm 37:*

c. *Rhythm 38*:

5 Rewrite *Rhythm 36* in $\frac{4}{2}$.

6 Rewrite *Rhythm 37* in $\frac{4}{8}$.

7 Tap the following pieces from the *Scorebook*.

Mañana (*Scorebook* 40)
Turn Me 'Round (*Scorebook* 54)

TERMS, SYMBOLS, AND CONCEPTS

syncopation
counting syncopated and nonsyncopated rhythms

CHAPTER TWELVE

Mixed Meter Some pieces of music feature changes of meter in quick succession. This type of rhythmic organization is called **mixed meter** and is often found in contemporary classical music, jazz, and music from certain parts of the non-Western world. In the following exercise, the basic pulse of the quarter note remains constant through several metrical changes, even though the number of beats per measure changes.

1 Tap *Rhythms 39–41* along with the cassette.

a. *Rhythm 39*:

b. *Rhythm 40*:

c. *Rhythm 41*:

2 Repeat *Rhythms 39–41* without tapping. Count the basic beat with each rhythm, as indicated.

a. *Rhythm 39*:

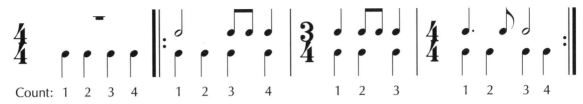

Count: 1   2   3   4   1   2   3   4   1   2   3   1   2   3   4

b. *Rhythm 40*:

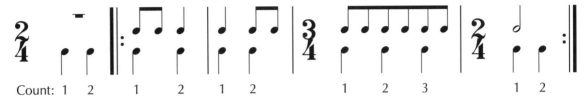

Count: 1   2   1   2   1   2   1   2   3   1   2

c. *Rhythm 41*:

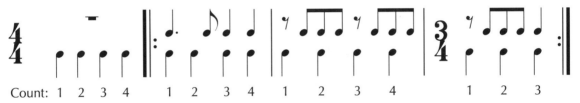

Count: 1   2   3   4   1   2   3   4   1   2   3   4   1   2   3

3 In each of the following exercises, write in the missing meters.

Example

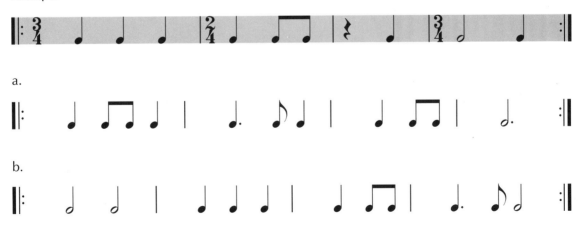

c.

d.

e.

Nonmetered Music

Not all music is written in metered form. In music without meter, there are no bar lines to set off regular metrical groupings. To understand **nonmetered music,** it is important to determine which note serves as the basic pulse, and then to follow that basic pulse throughout the rhythmic pattern. This way, each note receives the appropriate number of beats. In the following examples and in exercise #4, the quarter note serves as the basic pulse.

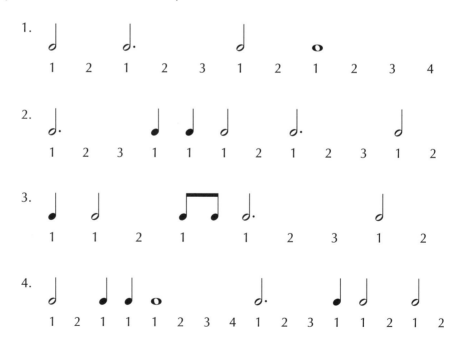

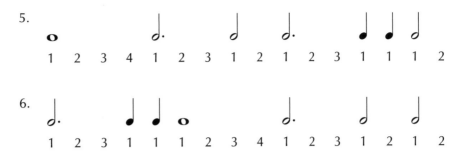

5.
1 2 3 4 1 2 3 1 2 1 2 3 1 1 1 2

6.
1 2 3 1 1 1 2 3 4 1 2 3 1 2 1 2

Counting the Basic Pulse

When counting nonmetered music, it is useful to mark where the basic pulse occurs (see p. 60), rather than writing in numbers. Imagining a pulse in this way is actually easier than counting the beats. For example, the rhythms given above can be treated in this way:

4 Write the basic pulse below the following rhythms, as in the examples above. Then tap each rhythm, keeping the basic pulse steady.

More Complex Meters

Throughout this book, we have focused on meters that feature two, three, or four beats per measure. Certain pieces of music, however, are based in meters that are more complex. These meters contain an uneven number of beats per measure; five and seven beats per measure are among the most common. One of the interesting aspects of meters in five or seven is that they divide into unequal groupings within the measure. You may hear a meter of five beats as a grouping of three followed by a grouping of two, or two followed by three. A meter of seven beats may divide into a grouping of three followed by a grouping of four, or four followed by three. The following examples present only a few of the many possible ways these meters sound.

5 Listen to *Rhythms 42–44* on the cassette. When you have become familiar with them, tap out the parts.

a. *Rhythm 42*:

b. *Rhythm 43*:

c. *Rhythm 44*:

6 Tap the rhythm of *Morena* (*Scorebook* 23).

TERMS, SYMBOLS, AND CONCEPTS

mixed meter
counting mixed meter
nonmetered music

counting nonmetered music
meter in 5
meter in 7

Appendix I

TABLE OF NOTE AND REST VALUES

The value of each of the following symbols is based on the quarter-note unit of one beat.

Name	Symbol	Value (in ♩'s)
whole note	𝅝	4
whole rest	𝄻	4
half note	𝅗𝅥	2
half rest	𝄼	2
dotted half note	𝅗𝅥.	3
dotted half rest	𝄼·	3
quarter note	♩	1
quarter rest	𝄽	1
eighth note	♪	1/2
eighth rest	𝄾	1/2
sixteenth note	𝅘𝅥𝅯	1/4
sixteenth rest	𝄿	1/4

Name	Symbol	Value (in ♩'s)
thirty-second note		$1/8$
thirty-second rest		$1/8$
sixty-fourth note		$1/16$
sixty-fourth rest		$1/16$

THE RELATIONSHIP OF NOTE VALUES TO EACH OTHER

Appendix II

RHYTHM SPACERS

Scorebook

I. Melodies from Around the World

1 *Lullaby*

Plains Apache

2 *Group Song*

West African

3 *Game Song*

Hungarian

4 *Fray Diego*

Spanish

5 *O du schöner Rosengarten*

German

6 *Brocham Lom*

Gaelic

7 *Oliver and the Maiden*

Icelandic

8 *Philis, plus avare que tendre*   **French**

9 *Die Gedanken sind frei*   **German**

10 *Song of the Crow*   **Chinese**

11 *Worksong*   **Chinese**

12 *Cherry Blooms*   **Japanese**

13 *Cradle Song*   **Japanese**

14 *Melody*   **Finnish**

15 *Que ne suis-je la fougère*   **French**

16 *Jeune fillette*   **French**

17 *O'er the Burn, Bessie*

18 *The Hunter*

Greek

19 *Carraig Aonair*

Gaelic

20 *In dem Weiten stand ein Haus*

German

21 *The Knife Sharpener*

Dutch

22 *Hymn*

Armenian

23 *Morena*

Portuguese

24 *Dream Song*

Scandinavian

II. Songs and Ballads

25 *I Know Where I'm Going*

Traditional

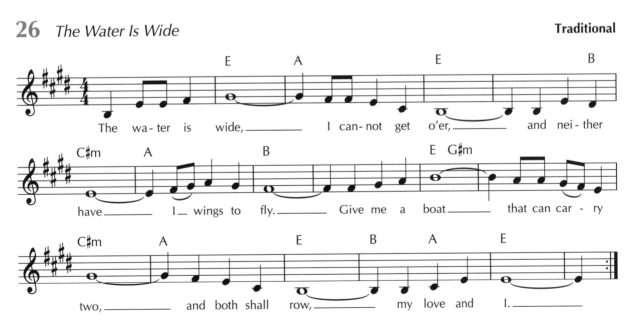

1. I know where I'm go-ing, and I know who's go-ing with me; I know who I love, but the dear knows who I'll mar-ry. 2. Feath-er beds are soft, and paint-ed rooms are bon-nie; But I would trade them all for my hand-some, win-some John-nie.

3. I have stockings of silk, and shoes of bright green leather;
   Combs to buckle my hair, and a ring for every finger.

4. Some say he's bad, but I say he's bonnie;
   Fairest of them all is my handsome, winsome Johnnie.

26 *The Water Is Wide*

Traditional

The wa-ter is wide, I can-not get o'er, and nei-ther have I wings to fly. Give me a boat that can car-ry two, and both shall row, my love and I.

2. I leaned my back against an oak,
   Thinking it was a trusty tree;

But first it bended and then it broke,
As thus did my true love to me.

27 *Barbrie Allen*

Traditional English

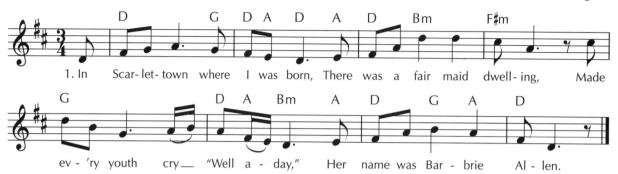

1. In Scar-let-town where I was born, There was a fair maid dwell-ing, Made

ev - 'ry youth cry __ "Well a - day," Her name was Bar - brie Al - len.

2. All in the merry month of May,
   When green buds they were swelling,
   Young Jonny Grove on his deathbed lay,
   For love of Barbrie Allen.

3. He sent his man unto her then
   To the town where she was dwelling:
   "You must come to my master, dear,
   If your name be Barbrie Allen."

4. So slowly, slowly she came up,
   And slowly she came nigh him,
   And all she said when there she came:
   "Young man, I think you're dying!"

5. He turned his face unto the wall,
   And death was drawing nigh him:
   "Adieu, adieu, my dear friends all,
   Be kind to Barbrie Allen."

28 *Drink to Me Only with Thine Eyes*

Traditional English

Words by Ben Jonson (1616)

Drink to me on - ly with __ thine eyes, __ And I __ will pledge with mine; ____

Or leave a kiss but in __ the cup, __ And I'll __ not ask for wine. ____ The

thirst __ that from the soul __ doth rise, Doth ask a drink __ di - vine: ____

But might I of Jove's nec - tar sup, __ I would __ not change for thine. ____

2. I sent thee late a rosy wreath,
   Not so much honoring thee,
   As giving it a hope, that there
   It could not withered be.

   But thou thereon did'st only breathe,
   And sent'st it back to me;
   Since when it grows and smells, I swear,
   Not of itself, but thee.

29 *The Trees They Do Grow High*   **Traditional**

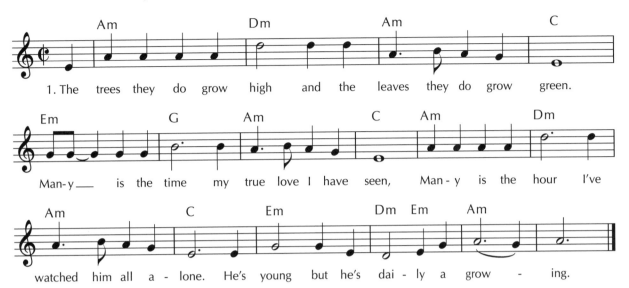

1. The trees they do grow high and the leaves they do grow green. Man-y __ is the time my true love I have seen, Man-y is the hour I've watched him all a - lone. He's young but he's dai - ly a grow - ing.

2. Father, dear Father, you've done me great wrong,
   You've married me to a boy who is too young.
   I am twice twelve and he is but fourteen,
   He's young, but he's daily a-growing.

3. Daughter, dear daughter, I've done you no wrong.
   I've married you to a great lord's son.
   He will make a lord for you to wait upon,
   He's young, but he's daily a-growing.

4. At the age of fourteen, he was a married man,
   At the age of fifteen, the father of a son,
   At the age of sixteen, his grave it did grow green,
   And death had put an end to his growing.

30 *Dear Willie*   **Traditional**

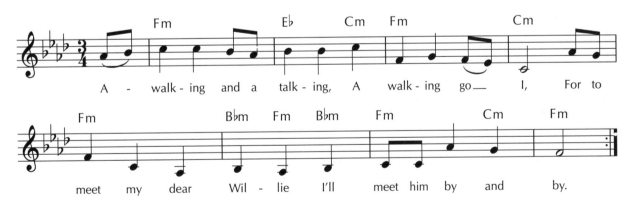

A - walk - ing and a talk - ing, A walk - ing go __ I, For to meet my dear Wil - lie I'll meet him by and by.

2. For to meet him is a pleasure, but parting is grief.
   And a false hearted lover is worse than a thief.

3. For a thief he will rob you and take what you have
   But a false hearted lover will lead you to the grave.

4. And the grave will consume you and turn you to dust
   Not one boy in twenty a poor girl can trust.

   (repeat first verse)

31 *Henry Martin*

Traditional

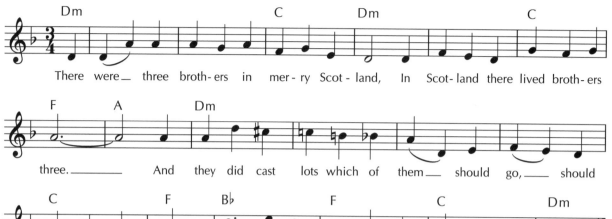

There were three brothers in merry Scotland, In Scotland there lived brothers three. And they did cast lots which of them should go, should go, should go, should go, For to turn robber all on the salt sea.

2. The lot it did fall upon Henry Martin,
   The youngest of all the three,
   That he should go, he should go, should go, should go, should go,
   For to turn robber all on the salt sea.

3. He had not been sailing a long winter's night,
   And part of a long winter's day,
   Before he espied a lofty stout ship, stout ship, stout ship,
   Come along down on him straight away.

32 *Sleep Gently*

American

from *The Calendar Songbook*
(used by permission)

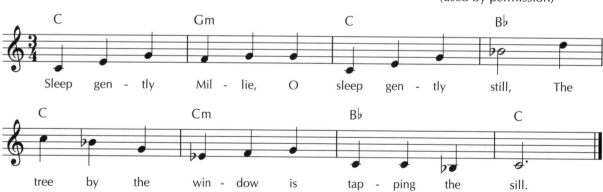

Sleep gen - tly Mil - lie, O sleep gen - tly still, The tree by the win - dow is tap - ping the sill.

2. Sleep gently Millie, oh sleep while you can,
   The rain on your garden is greening the land.

3. Sleep gently darling, the sun's still asleep,
   When it comes to peeking, I'll tickle your feet.

4. Quiet my sweet love, oh quiet this morn,
   Your garden is waiting, a new day is born.

   (repeat first verse)

33 Greensleeves

Traditional

A - las my love,— you do me wrong— to cast me off— dis - cour-teous-ly, And
I have lov - ed you so long, — De - light - ing in— your com - pa - ny.
Green - sleeves — was all my joy, ——— Green - sleeves — was my de - light,
Green - sleeves was my heart of gold— And who but my la - dy Green - sleeves.

2. I have been ready at your hand to grant whatever you desire;
   I have both waged life and land, your love and goodwill for to have.
   Greensleeves (etc.)

3. If you intend thus to disdain, it does the more enrapture me;
   And even so I still remain a lover in captivity.
   Greensleeves (etc.)

4. And yet thou wouldst not love me, thou couldst desire no earthly thing;
   Still thou hadst it readily, thy music still to play and sing.
   Greensleeves (etc.)

34 Johnny Has Gone for a Soldier

Traditional American

There I sat on But - ter-milk Hill, Who could blame me weep my fill, And
ever - ry tear would— turn a mill: John - ny has gone for a sol - dier.

2. Me, oh my, I loved him so,   And only time will heal my woe:
   Broke my heart to see him go,   Johnny has gone for a soldier.

35 *The Oak and the Ash*

Traditional English

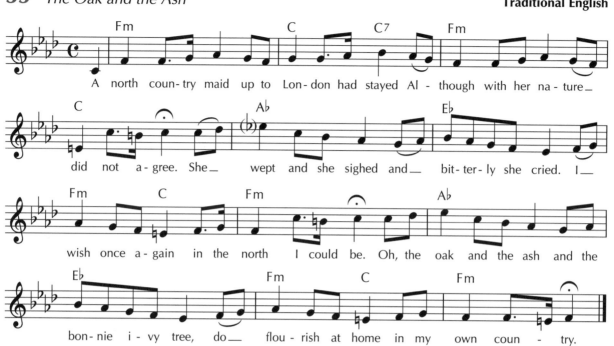

A north coun-try maid up to Lon-don had stayed Al - though with her na-ture

did not a-gree. She_ wept and she sighed and_ bit-ter-ly she cried. I_

wish once a-gain in the north I could be. Oh, the oak and the ash and the

bon-nie i-vy tree, do_ flou-rish at home in my own coun - try.

2. Oh, would I be in the North Country,
   Where the lads and the lassies are making the hay;
   I delighted to see what is dearest to me,
   When a mischievous light somehow took me away.
   Oh, the oak and the ash and the bonnie ivy tree,
   Do flourish at home in my own country.

3. At wakes and at fairs, being void of all cares,
   We there with our lovers did play and did dance;
   Then mistakenly I my fortune did try,
   And so to London my steps did advance.
   Oh, the oak and the ash and the bonnie ivy tree,
   Do flourish at home in my own country.

36 *La paloma*

Spanish

Es la Pa-lo-ma di - vi - na La que nun-ca tu-vo

man - cha, Pa - ra su-bir a su ni - do su dul-ce vue-lo le -

van - ta. Ma - rí - a Ma - rí - a lle-na de gra - cia.

(It is the divine dove, the one that never had a stain.
She takes sweet flight to reach her nest. Mary, Mary, full of grace.)

37   En el portal de Belén

Spanish Christmas song

En el por - tal_____ de Be - lén._____ Hay u -
na_ cu - na de vien - to._____ Es pa - ra me - cer al
Ni - ño._____ La no - che_ del_____ Na - ci - mien - to._____

(At the gates of Bethlehem, there is a cradle of wind.
It is to rock the child, the night of the birth.)

2. Los tres Reyes del Oriente
   Guiados por una estrella,
   Fueron a adorar al Niño
   Que nació de una doncella.

3. De María, Virgen pura,
   Nació Jesús Nazareno,
   Vino por borrar la culpa,
   Que dejó padre primero.

2. The three kings of the Orient
   Guided by a star,
   Went to adore the Child
   Who was born of a maiden.

3. Of Mary, pure virgin,
   Was born Jesus of Nazareth,
   Came to erase the sins
   Which were left by the first father.

38   Silent Night

Franz Gruber
(1787–1863)

Words by Joseph Mohn

Si - lent night, ho - ly night, All is calm, all is bright.
Round yon Vir - gin Moth - er and Child, Ho - ly In - fant so ten - der and mild,
Sleep in heav - en - ly peace,_____ sleep_ in heav - en - ly peace.

39 *Oh Freedom*

African-American spiritual and freedom song

Oh _____ free- dom, _ oh _____ free- dom, _ oh _____ free- dom o- ver me, _____ And be - fore I'll be a slave I'll be bur- ied in my grave And go home to my Lord and be free. _____

2. No more shackles, no more shackles, no more shackles over me,
   And before I'll be a slave I'll be buried in my grave
   And go home to my Lord and be free.

3. No more weeping, no more weeping, no more weeping over me,
   And before I'll be a slave I'll be buried in my grave
   And go home to my Lord and be free.

40 *Mañana*

Spanish

Ma - ña - na por _____ la ma - ña - na te _____ e - spe - ro Jua - na _____ en el ca - fé, _____ te ju - ro Jua - na que ten - go ga - nas de ver - te la pun - ta del pié, _____ te ju - ro Jua - na que ten - go ga - nas de ver - te la pun - ta del pié. _____

(Tomorrow in the morning I'll wait for you at the cafe.
I swear to you, Juana, that I want to see the tip of your foot.)

41 *Mañanitas*

Traditional Spanish

Es - tas son ___ las ma - ña - ni - tas que con - ta - ba el rey Da - vid. Hoy por

ser ___ dí - a de tus san - tos te las can - ta - mos a ti. Des -

pier - ta mi, bien des - pier - ta. Mi - ra que ya a - man - ne - ció Ya los

pa - ja - ril - los can - tan la lu - na ya se me - tió.

(This is the morning song that King David sang,
and today, since it's your birthday, we'll sing it for you.

Awake my sweet, awake. It's time to arise.
The birds are already singing, and the moon has gone.)

42 *Believe Me if All Those Endearing Young Charms*

Traditional

Words by Thomas Moore (1808)

Be - lieve me, if all those en - dear - ing young charms, Which I gaze on so fond - ly to -

day, ___ Were to change by to - mor - row, and fleet in my arms, Like ___

fair y gifts fad - ing a - way, ___ Thou wouldst still be a - dored, as this mo - ment thou art, Let thy

love - li - ness fade as it will, ___ And a - round the dear ru - in, each

wish of my heart, Would en - twine it - self ver - dant - ly still. ___

III. Canons, Rounds, and Part Songs

43 *Dona nobis pacem*

Traditional round

Do - na no - bis pa - cem, pa - cem, do - na___ no - bis pa - cem.

Do - na no - bis pa - cem, do - na no - bis pa - cem.

Do - na no - bis___ pa - cem, do - na no - bis pa - cem.

44 *Oh How Lovely Is the Evening*

Traditional German round

Oh how love - ly is the eve - ning, is the eve - ning,

When the bells are sweet - ly ring - ing, sweet - ly ring - ing,

ding___ dong ding___ dong ding___ dong.

45 *Hey, Ho, Nobody at Home*   **Traditional English round**

Hey, ho, no - bod - y at home,

Food nor drink nor mon - ey have we none,

Yet shall we be mer - - - - - ry. __

46 *The Welcome Song*   **Traditional American canon**

Wel - come, wel - come eve - ry guest, wel - come to our mu - sic fest.

Mu - sic is our on - ly __ cheer, fills both soul and __ ra - vished ear.

Sa - cred nine __ teach us the mood, sweet - est notes to __ be ex - plored.

Gen - tly moves the trem - bling __ air to __ com - plete our __ con - cert fair.

47 *Shalom Chaverim*

Traditional Israeli round

Sha - lom cha - ve - rim, sha - lom cha - ve - rim, sha - lom, sha - lom, Le

hit - ra - ot, le hit - ra - ot, sha - lom, sha - lom.

(Farewell good friends, farewell good friends, farewell, farewell,
'Til we meet again, 'til we meet again, farewell, farewell.)

48 *The Blue Note Canon*

from *Canons Old and New*
(used by permission)

The blue note sounds so __ blue __ I don't know why do __ you?

Why does the blue note sound so blue? Why does it sound __ so __ blue?

Blue note deep - est blue no one knows why it sounds blue.

49 *Planting Song*

from *The Calendar Songbook*
(used by permission)

1. Spring has come, it's time to — plant, time to plant the har - vest.
2. Seed to soil, it's one by — one. Who can seed the far - thest?

Win - ter now is — gone, And the win - ter's cold - ness.

Now the days grow — long, the sun shines now with bold - ness.

50 *Willie, Take Your Little Drum*

Burgundian carol

Wil - lie, take your lit - tle drum, With your whis - tle Ro - bin, come! When we hear the fife and drum, Tu - re - lu - re - lu pat - a - pat - a - pan, When we hear the fife and drum, Christ - mas should be — frol - ic - some.

51 Christmas Has Come

from *The Hirsau Book of Carols*
(used by permission)

1. Christ - mas has come and the snow's on the hill,
2. Door - ways now o - pen___ for ev' - ry guest,

Turn - ing no long - er, the si - lent mill; Al - le - lu - ia
All gen - tle peo - ple are now at rest;

be of good cheer, Al - le - lu - ia Christ - mas is here!

52 All the Stars

Traditional part song

from *The Hirsau Book of Carols*
(used by permission)

All the stars, turn with time; like an end - less rhym - ing.

All the earth, all the sky, up to heav - en climb - ing.

2. Day and night, night and day, dance with one another.
   Time and task, faith will last, once it is discovered.

3. Dark and light, all is right, when the stars are singing;
   Harmonies, always please; music, love is bringing.

   (repeat first verse)

53 *Ringing of the Bells* **Traditional part song**

from *The Hirsau Book of Carols*
(used by permission)

54 *Turn Me 'Round* **African-American freedom song**

IV. From the Classical Heritage

55 *Lullaby*

Johannes Brahms
(1833–1897)

56 Chorale Melody from *The Christmas Oratorio*

Johann Sebastian Bach
(1685–1750)

57 *Puer natus in Bethlehem*

J. S. Bach

58 Chorale Melody from *The Wedding Cantata*

J. S. Bach

59 *Ode to Joy* from *Symphony No. 9*

Ludwig van Beethoven
(1770–1827)

60 Theme from *Don Giovanni*

Wolfgang Amadeus Mozart
(1756–1791)

61 *Nancie*

Thomas Morley
(1557/8–1602)

62 *Galiarda*

William Byrd
(1543–1623)

63 *Minuet*

Henry Purcell
(c. 1659–1695)

64 *Minuet*

Robert Visée
(c. 1650–c. 1725)

65 *Sarabanda* from *Concerto Grosso*, Op. 6, No. 11

Arcangelo Corelli
(1653–1713)

66 Theme from *Concerto Grosso No. 5*

George Frederic Handel
(1685–1759)

67 Theme from *Symphony No. 103*

Franz Joseph Haydn
(1732–1809)

68 Theme from *Symphony No. 100*

Haydn

69 Theme from *Symphony No. 29*

Mozart

70 *Hunter's Theme* from *Der Freischütz*

Carl Maria von Weber
(1786–1826)

71 *Cujus animam*

Gioachino Rossini
(1792–1868)

72 *Study in C*

Ferdinando Sor
(1778–1839)

For guitar

73 *Minuet*   Mozart

74 Theme from *Piano Sonata No. 19* — **Beethoven**

75 Theme from *Symphony No. 6* — **Pyotr Il'yich Tchaikovsky** (1840–1893)

76 Prologue from *Prophetiae sibyllarum*

Orlando di Lasso
(1530/32–1594)

77 *Psalm 75*

Heinrich Schütz
(c. 1585–1672)

78 *Remember, O Thou Man*

Thomas Ravenscroft
(c. 1582–c. 1635)

A Christmas carol

O thou man, thy time is spent. Re - mem - ber O thou man,

O thou man, thy time is spent. Re - mem - ber O thou man,

O thou man, thy time is spent. Re - mem - ber O thou man,

O thou man, thy time is spent. Re - mem - ber O thou man,

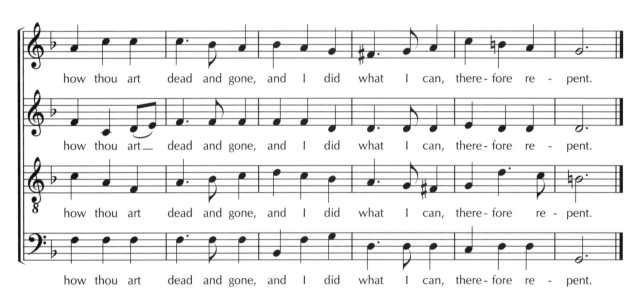

how thou art dead and gone, and I did what I can, there - fore re - pent.

how thou art dead and gone, and I did what I can, there - fore re - pent.

how thou art dead and gone, and I did what I can, there - fore re - pent.

how thou art dead and gone, and I did what I can, there - fore re - pent.

2. Remember God's goodnesse,
   O thou man, O thou man,
   Remember God's goodnesse
   And his promise made.
   Remember God's goodnesse,
   How he sent his son doubtlesse
   Our sinnes for to redresse, be not affraid.

3. The Angels all did sing,
   O thou man, O thou man,
   The Angels all did sing
   Upon Shepheards hill.
   The Angels all did sing
   Praises to our heavenly King,
   And peace to man living with a good will.

79   Chorale from *Cantata No. 43*

J. S. Bach